White Feather

A Collection of Poetry

by

CLARE M HEGARTY

authorHOUSE®

AuthorHouse™ UK
1663 Liberty Drive
Bloomington, IN 47403 USA
www.authorhouse.co.uk
Phone: 0800.197.4150

Published by AuthorHouse 08/29/2016

ISBN: 978-1-5246-6271-4 (sc)
ISBN: 978-1-5246-6270-7 (e)

Print information available on the last page.

Any people depicted in stock imagery provided
by Thinkstock are models, and such images are
being used for illustrative purposes only.
Certain stock imagery © Thinkstock.

This book is printed on acid-free paper.

In memory of my beloved mother Deirdre Margaret Hegarty
– Beautiful; both inside and out.
My inspiration, my heroine.

Preface

Diagnosed with cancer on 03rd June 2015, she bravely and humbly accepted that it was her time to leave us here on earth and watch over us from afar. She did not cry a single tear and remained dignified and ladylike until she slipped into an eternal sleep, just seven weeks later on 22nd July 2015, with her husband and us, her children, by her bedside. She died just as she lived; peacefully, surrounded by love. We miss her dearly every single day. For us, the grief is only just beginning. For the many other families who have borne the pain of loss before us and those who will do so after us, I hope this collection gives you strength and comfort knowing that the wave of grief will come but drowning in it is not the answer in coping with loss and pain.

I was never one to believe in "signs" or stories of "messages" from beyond the grave however I asked my mammy to let me know she was with me. On the morning she died I found my first white feather. I was taking a moment by myself to catch my breath and all of a sudden, out of nowhere a white feather floated onto my bed. This has been a consistent theme. At times when I need to ask her advice or I am trying to make a decision, there always seems to be a little white feather that floats into my path. I am comforted by the idea that she is letting me know she is with me.

I have documented my thoughts and feelings as I experienced them in the aftermath of losing the most important person in my life, in the hope that somewhere, someone's similarly painful journey is made that little bit easier.

ACKNOWLEDGMENTS

Gavin, Michael, Nicola, Lorraine, Patrick, Conall, Róise & Sebastian: The most amazingly strong, supportive, loving team. She would be so proud of each and every one of you and the great things you are achieving. I love you all so much and could never thank you for all you do for me! Here's to many more memories Team Higberts – I hope we never stop laughing. Conall it's your job to tell baby Róise (and any future little people!) how brilliant granny Deirdre was.

Fiona (Shoda): I know you are part of Team Higgs but you deserve to be singled out for having to put up with me on a constant basis. I know I don't always listen to you, but I thank you for being there to pick up the pieces when I make mistakes (which usually you have pre-empted!). You are my best friend dear sissy and I love you more than anyone else in this world. I'd be lost without you.

Daddy: Thank you for all the guidance and support (mainly financial!) over the years.

Clare Snr, Fr. Philip, Nuala & Joe, Lily, Noel & Catherine, Gen & Peter, Anne & the entire McKenna family: So proud to call you my family. You have always been there for mammy, daddy and us "four wains" throughout the years and we can never repay you for the love and support you have shown to us. So many happy memories.

Rosemary & Gerry: There are no words big enough to thank you for your endless love and support. You have been the light on many a dark day and we love you dearly.

Emma & Liam: I hate you both so much...best friends for life! Thank you for dragging me through 2015 and sticking by my side when I needed you - without me having to ask, y'ole devil. #clarecares

Orla, Kev, Laura, Gemma, Pauline, Amy, Danielle, Danielle, Claire, Colleen, Eoibhlin, Fiona, Rosie, Emma, and Deirdre aka "All the Lads": Here we are now... I don't know how I managed to find you all but I'm so glad I did. I love you all very much. Thanks for supporting me through this. Here's to making many more hilarious memories in the future – let's never lose touch guys.

To everyone else who has shown love and support to our family especially this past year; Philomena and the Hannaways, Emma & The Warren boys, The Kavanagh Family, The Faulkner Family, The McGinty Family, The McDaid Family, Grainne McAnaney (our turn to repay the support), the magical Rose Green and the Staff at Foyle Hospice, Dr Campbell & the staff at Glendermott Medical, Adele and the girls at Jon Paul's Salon, my dear friends Kirstie Mkhize, Mag (Mabel Liaw), Wee Bessy (Beth) O'Donnell, all my lovely ladies from the Speech & Language Therapy Team in Liverpool who have made me laugh through the tears on many an occasion, My

Liverpool mother Sue for the endless advice, hugs and all your proof reading, Katy Schreiber; my Liverpool Bestie and boxing legend Dee Taggart for letting me kick his ass.

For helping to make my vision a reality; Paul Hippsley (Guildhall Press), Marc Soal (iPrint Derry), The Derry Journal, Stephen Latimer Photography, Cruse Bereavement Care, Alexa Navarro (AuthorHouse), Kim Cavannah (AuthorHouse UK) Kevin Karl and all the staff at Authorhouse UK.

And finally to all of those people who have inspired me to create this collection; I am forever grateful to you all.

CONTENTS

INTRODUCTION

"Clare?"

"Aye mammy how'd you get on? What did he say?"

"They've found a mass. They think its cancer."

And that's the conversation which changed my life. Changed me. Changed my family. Changed reality. Changed my dreams. Changed my heart. Changed my thoughts. Changed my words. Changed my world.

Standing in the doorway to my room, on an ordinary Wednesday afternoon in June, everything changed.

I can remember the smell of her perfume still lingered on the landing and for what felt like half an hour, I felt the silence descend on the home that she had made for us. But inside I felt it brewing. A sense of mania. That fight or flight mode. I had to fight. I had to be strong.

Dear old friend depression had left me numb; unable to feel strong sense of emotion in recent times so I suppose this fiery reaction was good. This awakening making me feel like a human once again. Like someone. Someone I don't even recognise now.

I called everyone she loved and one by one dealt them the almighty blow. The dreaded c-bomb. I was cool. I was calm. I didn't shed one tear.

My younger sister came bounding through the door. She had driven from work in a state. She couldn't speak, barely breathe or function. She lay sobbing in a heap on the sofa, unable to form words, whilst I kept handing out the blows. Neither of us able to comfort one another. We just wanted her.

My brother in Doha could barely talk on the phone. My other brother in auto pilot. My sister in laws broke down at work. Aunties in a panic. Friends in shock. No one believing what I was telling them. Thinking it was another of my many pranks. There was nothing funny this time.

Daddy came through the door next. Paler than words can describe. And then the most beautiful woman I will ever lay my eyes on walked confidently through the living room door. Not a tear stain on her cheek. That tight lipped smile she gave when she didn't have anything to say. Our wee mammy. Our best friend came and hugged my sister and I and told us it would be ok. She was cool. She was calm. She didn't shed one tear.

I wanted in that very moment to just hold her and never let her go. I wanted to take her beautifully delicate hands in mine and keep them there forever.

Days and weeks flew by in a whirl as the mania continued to invade our home. Everyone was on a high, fielding the same questions a million times from well wishers, drinking copious amounts of tea with the never ending visitors, plastering on smiles and laughing along at stories we had heard so often we could act them out; everyone was trying to remain brave and positive. Afraid of the damage imagination could cause. When darkness fell, that's when I would lay awake. Alone. Thoughts dancing in my head. Circling round and around like painted ponies on a carousel wheel. It was this unknown that had the ability to shake me the most. We were all shaking inside. Well, all but one.

She was steady. Stable. To be in her presence was calming. I have never felt such admiration for a single being my whole life. I remember talking to Michael, my brother, one night and the only word we consistently used was "inspiration." Not in that obnoxious talk show host type way but watching her was genuine; so deeply inspiring. Like a gold fish swimming in the confinement of a glass bowl, she sat on the sofa in the corner of the living room while visitors came and cried and hugged and laughed and kissed. She wasn't fazed by any of it. She was strong for them all and made each and every visitor leave our home feeling blessed to have been in the presence of something so beautiful and at peace. As her body grew weaker and frailer, she continued to radiate calmness and serenity; a true testament to her faith.

The Raven

On yonder hill rests ragged rotting ruins
Peering o'er the landscape's cruel centre,
Discouraging passers-by.
Visitors no longer venture.
Where once wide scoping windows
Filtered particles of light,
Darkness now proudly penetrates
Victorious in day and night.
Among the decrepit remnants
An indigenous creature roves.
Guarding secrets buried deep
The ominous raven roams.
Intelligent, he knows his game.
Scavenging once bleak barren land
He cries out to the wolves.
A carcass he has found.
Wilfully waiting he swoops on the remains,
He's Careful to retrieve,
A simple trophy he can laud -
The innocent's eyes he's thieved.
With bright new eyes he sees the world
A dreary place no more.
Yet his memory still is haunted by
His place among folklore.
A goddess on a hero's shoulder
Transformed in afterlife.
He doesn't wish to see the light;
Prefers a world of strife.
Even though he had a chance
Escaping's not an answer.
He buries the eyes deep in the earth
He's bold and dark as cancer.
The raven, like a sentry guard
Is waiting for invasion.
He who dares disturb his peace
Shall face the deathly raven.

1

Old Man

What's your way of coping?
Do you bury yourself in whiskey and woe?
Do you cry yourself to sleep?
Do you lock yourself away?
Him? He does it all.
Whiskey burning on its entry to the soul
Blocks it out 'til he passes out.
Been here for a while.
In a room
With cold grey walls
And shuttered doors.
A lock without a key.
Here some time and no one knows
He had sheltered himself away from it all.

Couldn't bear to hear the sounds
Of chattering clattering busy streets,
Or feel the slinking slowing down of time.
But now in the emptiness
He feels nothing
Or nothing less than nothingness.
Loneliness
His love departed.
Truth ripples destructively through his bloodstream.
Every thought starts and ends with her
She's forever on his lips.

Dear Mother;
Take his hand and wrap it carefully in yours
Slowly, slowly pull him from the darkest depths of this hell;
No fires burn here, only embers rest.
You can carry him away.

Death.

A harrowing experience to live through.
It creeps up like a stealthy fox,
Ripping comfortable safety nets
Standing still now frozen clocks.
For time cannot move on or grow.
The body vessel bare
The Creator wants his creations back -
Surely that's not fair?
Last breath released so effortlessly
Like a slowly puncturing tyre.
Chest rising stops and then sudden peace
The eye's now lack their fire.
What's left behind, an empty shell
Was once so full of life
Stillness sets, dreaming ends
Endless sleep almost a disguise.
Loved ones gather round the bed
Sobbing broken hearted
Too young to leave, so much to see
New phase of life had started.
In every tear there lays a mound of pain
Falling, dripping, pouring down
Blurry figures shaking hands
The body rests in earthy ground.

And then the tears are locked away.
Visitors stop as dust settles in.
When hollowness presents itself
Death disappears;
Grief must begin.

Watery Grave

Your beautiful head bobbing about like a buoy
I push your soft brown curls back,
They've been masking the majestic
Golden flaked blue stones I've bathed in.
My head resting where your head rests.
Only the darkness as my shield.
I gasp.
Gaping harrowing holes where once lay everything I ever
needed.
Tears don't come now.
They're no use now.
Then the thing that throws me to the ocean bed;
That tiny freckle standing proudly on your nose
It's gone
Did I take that too?
I took everything else,
All that's good.
I pushed
Too hard
Too far
Too long.
Falling backwards
Trying to reach to you
Water bombarding every crevice like a sinking ship
I see you
Fading slowly
Drifting further away
Out of my reach
You're gone.
I'm alone.
Sunk back into the ocean
Surrounded by silence.

Passport

Stamps on a passport ; a reminder of places discovered

But to the wanderer they only exist to taunt

Of places not yet touched upon.

Love leaves lines on the heart like a road map.

Paths that have been walked by ghosts of past lovers.

Some roads more worn than others.

Deeper, longer intertwined with insignificant routes.

But right through the centre, a track that's been started is somehow desolate now.

No one's walking.

It's been abandoned at the aggressive hands of pain and sadness.

This road has many places it should go.

It should meander through the memories of august days and September nights.

When lovers flew through skies just to be near, just to be close.

When waking up was the safest part of the day.

The time when finger tips gently traced their way down delicate skin.

When golden flaked eyes glistened in the first rays of a new day.

When soft perfect lips found the comfort of the necks slight hollow.

And there, in the glow of the fiery sun, two bodies passionately moved as one.

One lover will fight for the abandoned road to once again feel the tread of synchronised pairs,

Walking side by side, hands fitting perfectly together.

A comfort in the knowing their journey isn't over.

Like stamps on a passport, a reminder of where they were and where they are going.

Love leaves lines on the heart; this line will be never ending.

<u>Blanket</u>

In the stillness of the night
When the moon is surrounded by the comfort of the stars.
When the hustle of the city has died
And darkness infiltrates the room
Like a melody on the mind.

Winter winds whisper through the walls
A chill descends.
Awake.
Thinking thoughts that bring it bounding back.
Thoughts of past regrets stinging in the deepest chambers
of the chest.

Your face.
Still stimulating shivers.
Afraid to move, afraid to breathe,
Afraid to make you leave.
It's freezing here now.
But I feel its time.

Strip the blanket I've been hiding under from one month to
the next
It's so light now; o longer feeling like armour.
I look at all the holes - each one attributed to you.
You're the catalyst I needed.
You helped the world tear through
And pull me from the dark abyss.
I have nothing left to hide.

I give you the blanket.
You wrap it round your shoulders and you're warm.
You don't need to worry.
When winter winds lament around your body, I'm not far
away.

Butterflies

There's the old familiar butterflies

Fluttering freely, frantically inside.

Trying to escape.

Their aim?

To find you.

Searching, hoping in vain that you still want to feel

Their warm, exciting embrace surging through your body.

These stunning creatures

- a sign that there's still feelings.

There is still desire.

There is still hope

We are still something.

The hard exterior of the sheltering cocoon has now been penetrated.

The tiny butterflies dancing delicately.

They need to know you want them.

You,

Stunning creature;

I will love you into oblivion

My dear

You will flutter when you feel it.

Teeny Tiny Little Pill

Teeny tiny little pill
Oh will she let you in?
She wonders what would happen
If the blade would pierce her skin.

Vibrant blood comes seeping out
And trickles down her fingers
Dripping onto crisp white sheets
The gin haze stops to linger.

On the pillow next to her
Fine black thread doth lay
Just enough to close the hole
And take the pain away.

Tear stained cheeks without a sound
No one would know she's crying
She paints a smile and robots through
Empty eyes, a clue she's lying.

Bleeding ceased, gin wearing off
Pounding, penetrating pressure
Confusion clouds her manic mind
She stumbles from bed to dresser.

Opening the drawer she takes a box
From it removes a watch
Face furnished by faded leather straps
She fumbles with the catch.

Slips it on her slender wrist
She doesn't feel a pain
Looking down, the thread is gone
Her skin is whole again.

No scars to see, no blood stained hand
Was it all a dream?
A picture playing out for her
With death, the final scene.

Purposefully heads to the kitchen
And there beside the sink
Teeny tiny little pill
She doesn't need to think.

Wash it down and let it work
Magically balancing her head.
And so she's calm and thinking straight
Thankful she's not dead.

The Ghost

And so another sleepless night has thrust itself upon me,

Forcefully arousing creativity.

Waiting for the copper kettle to cry,

I inhale the sweet aroma of vanilla undertones from the candles

Glowing defiantly like beacons warning ships of stormy seas.

But not tonight.

No storms or waves I must battle to overcome.

Tonight feels different.

An atmosphere of anticipation clinging to the air.

Hopefully hanging on for happiness.

Listening as the passage of time appears

A steady heartbeat

Unaware that the world has stopped to rest its weary head.

I am not alone.

My favourite time of day

That time when I feel you all around me.

As memories flood my mind I let them pour from my mouth

Like a salivating dog, hungry with excitement.

Oh no!

Recalling moments I made you laugh;

Stimulates stinging sorrowful feelings somewhere inside.

It was quick tonight.

Pain powered through

Triumphantly overshadowing the joy of your company.

You don't like to see me jaded so you lead me off to bed

And tuck me in just like a child.

Place your lips upon my cheek. Kissing the imprints you've laid all these years.

You whisper to me "night night god bless."

My eye lids are heavy now as I peacefully drift off to a place where everything is as it was before.

And you…. you're immortal.

Chemicals Imbalanced

Chemicals imbalanced

Can't shake this sadness

Crawling like maggots

Feasting on madness

Too reliant on tablets

Memory's so callus

Flaunting your absence

Confidently anxious

Opinion of the masses

People so classless

Believing in status

Admiring propagandists

Disguising nonsense as gallant

Out to preserve

Reputation; the nerve

Give them what they deserve

Let them all stare

Don't really care

The lows cant compare

To a happiness that's rare

Laughing reaches the eyes

Lights in the sky

Not the day to die.

White Feather

Floating by like pretty bubbles in the air
Carelessly drifting in and out
You're all around.
Never one for grand dramatic gestures
Your ladylike presence; so simple, yet so powerful.
When the weight of the world bears down upon my already
aching head
And my heart is heavy with your memory
My arms feel empty but the muscles still recall the
contours of your embrace
And my fingertips still tingle at the preservation of the
smoothness of your perfect hands.
I open up my fraught frantic mind
Trying to accept that your body can't be next to me.
Your voice shall never speak new words.
Your sweet homely scent waiting to be triggered in my
misty mind
By stimulating strangers.
You're travelling with the wind now.
Gently gliding on the freshness of the crisp morning frost.
Feels almost like your breath awakening my senses.
Wind the window down, raspy acoustic songstress blaring
boldly
And there you are, next to me.
All around me as swirling breezes whisper my name
You call to me.
And from out of nowhere floats your physical form -
Simple white feather.

Summertime Sadness

It's another sunny Sunday in this paradise.

Bathed in the warmth of the glorious sun

Semi naked bodies gracefully disappear in and out of the clear blue water

Cooling the tiny trickles of sweat, breaking bolding on their brows.

The yellowy sand, so soft and silky

Moulding round the body like a baby cradled in swaddling clothes.

Sinking slowly until it's safe to rest a while.

Dogs intently chasing sticks, oblivious to the beauty all around.

Children's laughter lingers with the breeze, innocent and free

Mysterious castles made with wonder -

Their expansive moats protecting from the lapping waves.

Everyone is here.

Grandparents sitting in the shade, in sneaky slumbers behind dark glasses

Lovers linking hands as they create synchronised patterns along the water's edge,

The waves encircling their tanned feet, inviting them to play.

Pretty girls flaunt their figures in skimpy bikinis

Aiming to attract the attention of surfers striding bare chested towards them.

Faint bouquets of heather almost masked by cooling coconut cream.

An exciting season to see.

I sit up in the deserted dunes and try play out our scenes.

Writing in the hope these words might reach you.

Pouring out unfiltered thoughts filled with raw emotion.

My pen is full of you.

My mind contaminated by recollections of the lines on your forehead;

Lines I read like novel

My view now obscured with the cloudy haze of smoke.

As the aroma of smouldering coals infiltrate my nasal passages

Music fills the air as nonchalant teens circulate a fiery pit.

I tear these pages from my book and throw them on the fire.

Burning, curling, crumbling before my eyes

I watch the ashen words drift upwards to the sky.

These words might reach you one day

For we are under the same sky.

The Oyster and The Pearl

Bulbous glass with a long thin stem rests perfectly in the palm of my hand.

Beautiful deep floral bouquets drifting from the rich, velvety liquid inside.

Swirling it around and around and around, transfixed.

I exist just as I should tonight –in the present.

In the presence of new friends.

The mind is mellow but the heart is mad.

Madly passionate at memories of before.

I've always had romanticised ideals of love,

Man and women; husband and wife breeding pretty little children.

But life got in the way.

Those ideals still ever present with a reality so far from stereotype.

I love you in all your womanly glory.

I would drive to you through mountainous peaks in the dead of night

Just to wait for morning - your feminine virtue shines brightest with the sun.

Yet I accept it might never be this way again.

Romance relies on truth, a concept I concealed

Behind the sparkle of a smile.

She approaches me, this pretty, blonde young thing.

Not my thing.

You're my thing.

They all don't understand her, she reveals –

Pretty little girl in a shitty little world.

Placing her hand on my naked flesh, I'm cold.

Passionate flames a distant memory.

Tossing hair reveals tiny pieces of colourful art

Forever embalmed.

I will never be the cat who gets the birds.

Why have the oyster when you've already had the pearl.

Firefly

Never could I imagine another's touch would stimulate my senses

Thoughts of hands in mine that didn't belong to you seemed alien.

She came along like a firefly playing in the soft glow of the distant light

- I went towards her light.

It was raining; thirst quenching drops of rain poured down my face

So that no one could see the tears

Washing away any evidence of your existence.

Here I was, bathed in her new glow,

I was hooked on how free I felt.

No guilt or pain or worry or fear

I recognised this person standing in the rain.

And so I danced

With her

And I felt alive.

She took the blue out of the sky and painted the sparkle back in my eyes.

I put her on as my winter coat.

She could keep anything out;

The cold, the rain, the pain and you.

Wild Purple Mountain Flowers

"She saved you? Remember when I saved you?

How about you save yourself?!"

Oh little girl...

You see it only through the rose tinted, narcissistic frames
that furnish your face.

You see your actions favourably, fruitful in the fight to free
yourself

From this harrowing hell we are hurtling towards.

But then that's what falling apart does to one's mind and
soul and heart.

Bitterness and blame like tsunami waters wash away
compassion and care

Well I, my dear,

I can't say I care.

I let you hold me hostage; engorge my mind and taint my
memory with your negativity for too long.

They had warned me of this side.

Of the childlike way you could use my heart strings to
playfully swing

You'd spend hours climbing though my manic mind frame.

Pushing me away for the wrong I had done.

I'm no saint, yet nobody's fool.

Pulling me back when fresh new eyes laid upon me.

Eventually the keys stopped tinkling our tune.

You see, little girl...

It's your words that hurt the most.

Words whispered on a wire tongue.

I save myself.

Her parting left me cold and empty.

A dark, cold, empty shell; incapable of functioning in your world.

Yet the curtains of cloud parted.

Unveiling hope

That it would be alright

That she is watching

Her gentle hand resting on my shoulder – guiding me to make things right.

I want her to be proud

So I save myself

Over and over every day

For her.

It's all for her.

Ode to Whoever

A hero on a golden pedestal
Unreachable to nonentities;
Untouchable.
Respect reciprocated.
Reaching levels of loyalty
That one can only imagine.

The king to her queen
Purest love ever seen
Eternity seemed real.

Dreams of heroic rescues;
Pulled from dark depths of one's own mind
A hero's hand always there
To hold
To guide
To steady.

Waiting to cushion the falls
To fix broken walls
The hero heals it all.

But what if...
If he lies.
Looks in the eyes and lies.
Deliberately destroys the truth.
Mocking memories, taunting tragedy...
Hero no more

She predicted the fall
Results of alcohol
He blew it all.

Booze for breakfast
Liquid lunch
After dinner chasers.
Always an excuse
Replacing human emotions
Actually; just replacing humans.

Still continues to lie
No more fake tears to cry
Insides rot... they soon will die.

The Circus

I'm supposed to hold my tongue
Sure what would I know? I'm only young...
Looking down the barrel of my loaded gun;
I'm ready to take aim
Fire...
It's done.

And I would feel no sorrow or regret
I'd be free - a concept I forget
How it feels to live without pressure and debt
Of a perfect picture they expect.

I think about it when I'm alone;
Which is so often now; I have no home.
Forever wandering, wondering I'll roam
Without even the luxury of a thought to call my own.

I think I'll stop relying on the lobotomy pills
They tell me to take because my head is "ill."
Controlling raging winds; be still
Rapid wild fire - let me decide the kill.

Could I end my own misery - like a tired old mutt?
Just surviving, not living. An end to this rut?
Slow and obscene from a precise little cut?
Or avoid the scenic routes - take the shortcut.

Maybe writing it all down will help make a little sense.
Of the contrived advice from professional soap box
peasants,
Thinking it's cool to fit a tabloid taboo which misrepresents
A reality so real - not just another medical expense.

But I'm supposed to hold my tongue
"You've got everything and you're still young..."
Looking down the barrel of my loaded gun
I'm ready to take aim...
Fire
I'm done.

And so it is...

Driving through the wintery morning fog

Alone.

Silence pierced only by my lamenting sobs,

It hit me hard.

The penny thudding as it dropped,

Resonating completely in my once eccentric head space.

Cloudy images played out through the tears

As I recalled all that we had been through since you left.

You made life unbearable to live without you.

Loneliness and anger – my greatest companions.

Even though surrounded by familiar faces and voices, it all felt numb.

Everyone treading water at different depths

But united in our wait.

Waiting for the wave to come.

My story different from his story, different from her story, different from their story.

How does one know when they're ready for acceptance?

It's not an easy feat to admit finality.

Fear is an awful emotion to accept;

Once we let fear in, it pollutes like a cancer. Oh the irony!

And so that morning, in the lanes of unrelenting traffic, I finally felt it come.

Dear old fear my friend.

Like a predator it feasted on the corners of my mind,

Lavishing lingering hopes you were coming home,

Destroying dreams of you calling me, now confused with reality,

Fear found its home and settled there...deep within my soul.

And then I knew

You had gone.

* * *

I cried tears as big as raindrops

Dripping down hoping I would drown in them.

You had gone!

Jesus Christ you had really gone!

I'd live my life without my mother.

Without your warm hugs waiting when I came home.

Without your bright beautiful laugh when I'd remind you of our funny memories.

I'd never see you roll your eyes at my latest wildest pipe dream

Or touch your hand, or breathe you in.

Who'd be there to fix it all when I screwed it up again and again (and again)...

* * *

The tears kept coming as acceptance held me tight.

And so it is...

You exist now only in my dreams and in my memories.

Forever in my heart.

Thinking Out Loud

I look at how you held me when I was just a child;
You would wrap me in your loving arms
You soothe me when I cried.

Growing up throughout the years you were truly my best
friend.
I could tell you almost anything
On you I always could depend.

You gave everything you possibly had to make sure we
would succeed
Supporting us in every way;
Though we sometimes made you peeved!!!

When I went off to uni and spent money like the Beckhams;
You never left the Ulster bank
Giving me money for books.... not mayhem!

I tricked you into sending me to Barbados, as part of my
degree.
You were calm when you found out the truth –
You didn't murder me!

When I moved to Singapore and needed surgery to fly
home;
You put your fear of flying aside
And made sure I wasn't alone.

When I rang and told you I'd bought a dog and was bringing
home to Derry
You bit your tongue and adopted him,
When I moved to England on the ferry.

I'd ring you every single night just to talk about our day
I loved how I could make you laugh
More so at the ridiculous things I'd say.

When you said you were dying and there was nothing they could do,
I thought it was a bad dream;
life couldn't function without you.

As I watched you fade away and I could hold your hand no more;
I didn't have your words to fix this pain
To make my heart stop feeling sore.

I can't believe it's been a year since I last touched your face
These memories and photographs
Can never take your place.

You promised you would send us signs you were in heaven up above
And just when I need you most
I always feel your warmth and love.

Missing you seems to never cease, it gets harder everyday
But I find comfort knowing that you're here with me
Please never go away.

Untitled Message

Absence is prominent with time passing quickly
Nothing feels right, always something missing.
Milestones and experiences we wished you were sharing
You'd make it all better, always so loving and caring.

The baby has come, hope and joy she did bring
You've held her first, lullabies you would sing
As you rocked her in your arms, close to your heart
We're so glad you two met, right from the start.

Your wee blue eyed boy is chatting away
He tells us you're sleeping; kisses your picture each day.
You'd have so much fun together, he always made you smile
He misses you singing and dancing in your funny granny
style.

I took your advice and I started to write
And I've stayed out of trouble, my halo's still bright!
I'm trying to be just like you and make you so proud
Although I've not mastered your volume tips, I'm still
pretty loud.

Your two big sons are trying to soldier through
But it gets really hard as they're really missing you.
The house feels empty when they call in at lunch time
No sandwiches waiting with a mug of tea and a smile.

Now who did you think would crumble and fall?
Well she is fighting hard and showing us all
That you are with her every step of the way,
She's "stronger than we thought" - you always did say.

Don't you be worrying I made a promise to you;
That I would look out for her and help get her through.
That I'll stand beside her on her wedding day
And hold her hand, hoping the pain away.
The void will be massive without you by her side
But I'll read her the words you wrote as you died.

There are many who have gone through this similar pain
So many more will face it again and again.
Nothing can ever be normal in a world without the face
Of the person you love dearly, that no other can replace.

Everything soon changes and days don't feel the same
But you find yourself fighting, pushing through the pain.
Waking up and they're not there somehow feels like a dream
Yet as time continues to pass, you no longer need to
scream.

You soon stop blaming everyone and the anger starts to fade
Reality settles in as new normalities are made.
Talking, laughing, keeping memories alive
Will help you make it to the brighter side.
Hold and cherish those you love every single day
You never know when it will all fade away.

Afterword

The weeks and months which followed the death of my mother now seem like a blur. I read over this collection of poems and realise the ways in which I have adapted and grown and learned to cope in the face of pain; a pain that I cannot describe. I have watched the ways pain and grief have affected those who were touched by my mother and how the loss of her in our lives has changed us all. Some of us have dealt with it in a positive way, some in a creative way and then there are those who have avoided dealing with it at all. As I reflect on my journey throughout this experience thus far, I question some impulsive decisions I made, some relationships which I selfishly started or neglected and indeed some of my actions, however I have no regrets. The trials of this past year have strengthened me in ways I never deemed possible.

Until June 2015 I honestly believed that she was indestructible. That she would be there always for me to ring every night just to tell her about my day, to play pranks on her when I was bored (like the time I rang her and put on an accent, asked to speak to Mr. Sebastian Hegarty and she actually responded "Oh I'm terribly sorry Mr Sebastian is a dog!"), for her to be there when I came home from England with a big pot of homemade soup on and the warmest, strongest hug that made everything better. I believed that she would be there to for the big stuff like buying a house, getting married and hopefully starting my own family. Never did I imagine that she would be gone before any of this could happen.

But that's the truth which death brings with it. We are born to die. Death comes with inevitable change and I have learned through this experience the importance of accepting change. Everyone has their story; their experience of grief and loss. This has been mine.